Investing in Rental Properties

Buy, Rent, Sell, Repeat

by

Taylor K. McNeil

Table of Contents

Conclusion

Legal Notes

Introduction

Photo by Jesse Roberts on Unsplash

Congratulations on downloading *Investing in Rental Properties: Buy, Rent, Sell, Repeat* and thank you for doing so. The following chapters will discuss all great outcomes there are for buying a rental property including its many tax benefits, capital and equity gains, its retirement savings potential, and how owning a property allows you to handle your own investments, among many others. Real estate investing can be a great vehicle for diversifying your investment portfolio, and they are relatively safe regarding stability and returns because as long as there are people, housing will be in demand. If you can afford to invest in property now, payoffs will be worth it in the future if you can find and purchase an appealing home.

So many homes are out there right now available for the taking, and there are endless possibilities still left to be built. These homes are very flexible to when it comes to what you want to do with the property. Living in the home as your main residence for a year or two before you decide to rent it out or sell it will help you get a feel for the house so when the time comes to pass it along you will know all of its little quirks, and positives things to point out. Buying an investment rental property can be a huge deal for some people, while other people find that immediately after buying their first property they will decide that they love investing this way and want to buy 4 more properties over the next two years. Whether you decide you want to be a hands-on landlord or a passive property owner that relies on a property manager, you will find tips and tricks in this book aimed at helping you manage your investment property the way that fits in best with your life.

There are also many ways to invest in real estate: single-family homes, condominiums, duplexes, apartment complexes, retirement homes, and a whole slew of commercial property investment options. This book will help you determine which avenue is best for you investment based on your personal financial goals and long-term wealth projection and needs.

We will cover all the steps to the buying process from conducting your research about areas and location amenities, things to look for in potential homes, financing your property, and creating a strategy for managing your home and growing your rental property portfolio if that's the way you choose to continue growing your investments. What do you do after you have purchased your new investment rental property? Rent it out of course! Renting out your property takes a lot more work than just hoping a great tenant will magically fall into your lap. Advertising your property, screening potential tenants, and responding to their needs and requests requires a lot of time and due diligence, and to be honest we are not all cut out for being a landlord.

Managing your money once you've decided to invest is another very important aspect that will be covered in later chapters. Find out your net worth, cash flow projections, and learn why it is important to keep your rental property finances separate from your personal finances for your own financial longevity and health. Another important aspect is to know and become familiar with your credit score- this number can greatly affect your ability to qualify for a loan and the interest rate that comes with it will be tied to that number. We will talk later about how you can see what your score is and what kind of number you should shoot for before you apply for a loan.

Also covered in this book are the steps you will need to take to sell your property and make a profit if that's the way you want to go on to continue buying, renting, and selling real estate, and then turning around and doing it all again. We are excited to help you navigate through this fun time in your life that has all kinds of potential. We hope that while reading through this book you have made up your mind about your future regarding investment real estate. Whether this is your first time straying into real estate investment or if you are a seasoned pro, we hoped you learned something in this book that will help you in your future purchase, management, and sale of a property to help you maintain financial health, wellness, and stability.

There are plenty of books on this subject on the market, thanks again for choosing this one! Every effort was made to ensure it is full of as much useful information as possible, please enjoy!

Chapter 1: Why Should You Buy a Rental Property?

Photo by Julián Gentilezza on Unsplash

There is an ever-growing list of benefits one can see from investing in rental properties, and some of the most profitable benefits come from receiving tax-free growth, tax-free cash flow, and tax-free exchanges. This mix of equity growth and cash flow can help make you wealthier and strengthen your net worth all while you are continuing to purchase properties and grow your portfolio. There is a difference though between purchasing real estate as an investment, or if you want to pursue real estate as a business. House flipping dominates reality TV, but in reality, rental homes, not flipped homes are where the money can be found; homes generally appreciate over the years, but there's nothing better than receiving a steady monthly income from rent payments, and over the years you can increase those payments based on the area and the market.

When you invest in real estate you not only want to make a living, you also need to build wealth for the future. You will learn how to quickly find quality investments, purchase them, and resell them for a profit either in as-is condition or after fixing them up with basic cosmetic changes, also known as flipping houses. A monthly income from rental properties will quickly earn you profits that will be worth the money you spent and the time and energy it takes to manage the property. If stocks and bonds are not your thing, or if you are not seeing the kind of returns you want with more traditional investment options, a rental property could be a great alternative to expand and diversify your portfolio.

Tax-free growth

Making monthly payments on a rental property mortgage increases your equity ownership, and that will continue to grow if the housing market stays healthy. The Internal Revenue Service does not count your properties as capital gains until they are sold meaning your money will continue to accumulate and grow as long as it stays invested in the property. Great rental properties can generate compound tax-deferred growth that can be pocketed in advance by taking out a second mortgage or refinancing your mortgage with a larger amount- in both of these examples the cash-out deal is tax-free. Also, when you go to sell your home, if you decide you want to buy another investment rental property you won't be taxed on the sale of the home.

Tax-free cash flow

Taxes only have to be paid on the profit you make from your rental properties; to calculate this amount, add up all of your rental property income and subtract all of your expenses which can include things like mortgage interest, repairs, property taxes, and property management fees. Depreciation is a natural part of owning anything, but that depreciation can be written off a portion of the property's purchase price each year.

Residential real estate is said to have a depreciation timeline of about 27.5 years, so even if you do not spend any money, expenses still accrue- but those expenses can be used to offset taxable income and save money. The higher the tax rate, the more taxes you should be saving. Depreciation can be a benefit in real estate because properties are usually bought with debt. Under President Regan, laws were passed that changed depreciation expenses to be deductible under other passive income. Exceptions to this rule include claiming a $25,000 exemption if you earn below $100,000 a year and actively participate in the oversight of your rental, you or a spouse qualify as a real estate professional, or the year you sell the property you can deduct all of the passive rental loss from that year.

Tax-free exchanges

If you buy a rental property and then sell it, the IRS allows you to use those profits to invest in more rental property if you structure the sale as a tax-deferred exchange. The IRS does not see this type of transaction as a sale, so no tax payments will have to be paid on the exchange.

A 1031 tax-free exchange will allow you to avoid the capital gains tax by allowing you to trade one property for another without having to pay taxes on the exchange. This means that you can take all of the profits from your first property and reinvest them into your next property both maximizing the growth and compounding your investments. However beneficial this may be, expensive fees and an inflexible process make a 1031 exchange more difficult to execute.

Savings for retirement

Photo by Katarzyna Grabowska on Unsplash

Another benefit is the long-term returns of purchasing rental properties which makes them a reliable choice for your retirement account. Steady and predictable income coming in every month from your properties with before mentioned tax benefits is a great way to financially prepare for your retirement. Advances in healthcare are allowing people to live much longer causing them to ask: will I have enough saved for all of my expenses? Pensions are a thing of the past, and the age to receive Social Security has gone up five years, causing seniors to scramble to amass a larger reservoir of savings, also known as wealth building.

Traditional numbers suggest saving about 25x your annual expenses to be able to remain financially independent during retirement. With the normal way to invest including a portfolio of stocks, bonds, and mutual funds, the rule of thumb is to withdraw no more than 4% of your investment portfolio yearly, and that is assuming that the 4% is a combination of interest, compounded dividends potentially the sale of some assets.

The best way to see a consistent return on your investment is to buy properties with little risk and apparent predictability. Purchasing single-family homes in quality neighborhoods, especially those that already have their mortgages paid off reduces your risks and increases your income. Single-family homes tend to attract tenants that stay longer, pay on time, and are mostly self-sufficient, making them great targets for retirement investors. These types of homes that are also located in a good neighborhood are more likely to increase in value with inflation over time making them even more profitable.

Those looking to buy rental properties for retirement should begin to prioritize the long-term growth of their wealth. Increasing your savings for retirement can leave you extra money after paying your expenses to donate to a charity, leave wealth for your children and grandchildren, and prepare for any unknown expenses. Real estate investment is also great for lump-sum payouts which can be used to purchase more rental properties or go toward your retirement; when you sell your property, your payout will be the original cost of the home minus how much the home has increased in value during the years of your ownership and minus the capital gains tax you will owe on the sale.

If an emergency comes up after you've put in your time working and you are worried about taking funds out of your retirement accounts, one option to avoid that is to take out an equity loan. If you own a property but don't want to sell or you are not ready to sell, there is the possibility of borrowing against the property's worth. This amount is not considered as income so you will not need to pay that amount back with interest. If you pass away in possession of the property, your children or grandchildren will not have to pay capital gains tax on the property whether it has increased in value or not since the time of purchase. These assets are still subject to taxes on the estate- all the way up to almost $5.5 million dollars.

Managing your own property and money investments

When you purchase a rental property, you can decide to manage the property yourself, or hire someone to do that for you. If you are a control freak or just like things to be done a certain way, acting as your own property manager could be a great choice for you. Some things to consider if you are thinking about managing your own properties are:

- **You must keep up with the property's maintenance**
    - o Not only is there a landlord-tenant law that holds you responsible for keeping the property up to certain health and safety standards but keeping the property nice to retain or enhance its value is also worth your time! General maintenance can include making sure water, sewer, and trash are accessible to your tenants, and it can also deter future potential renters if they see a home that is lacking repairs and is slowly falling apart.
    - o The landlord-tenant law can also help investors find a structure for streamlining your management process. A good example would be adhering to the rules pertaining to security deposits: how much can you collect from a tenant, and when you must return their deposit are outlined as part of the law. Local and statewide tenant rules vary so pay attention to the laws in your area.

- **Beware of tenant turnover**
    - o Keeping your tenants happy is the best way to prevent turnover. One way to do this is to respond quickly to repair requests, or if you own a rental property like an apartment complex, make sure that the new tenants you put in next door to your old tenants are of equal caliber. Rental rates are predicted to increase in the current market as housing prices go up and

people cannot afford to own their own home; while you can't increase a tenant's rent during the term of their lease, it's fair game to increase it when their lease is ending and they want to renew with you. In the end, don't be afraid to turn down potential tenants because you are afraid you won't find any others to replace them.

- **Pay your taxes**
  - Properly managing your financial obligations is a big component of successfully managing your properties. Since your management of the property is considered a business, you can often deduct home office expenses and other depreciation expenses mentioned earlier in the chapter that you are allowed to take. The best way to ensure proper operating financial books would be to hire an accountant that specialized in investment property law.

- **When in doubt, hire a property manager**
  - Sometimes managing properties can be overwhelming and time-consuming if you have another job to work. Finding a property manager is not cheap, but it is a big decision that could pay off if you find the right person to entrust the job with. Remember, not everyone is cut out to deal with tenants, just like not everyone is cut out for customer service; if you don't particularly enjoy interacting with people, a property manager would be the best bet for you.

- **Set yourself up for success by being organized**
  - When the time comes you will be held accountable for everything regarding your rental property: collecting rent, signing leases, paying taxes, and conducting maintenance if you decide to not go with a property manager. Set up systems and processes for these items as well as how to screen tenants, document expenses,

and put aside time to periodically visit the property and conduct a walk-through inspection. Technology can be your friend in this regard- scan and store records, receipts, emails, etc. electronically to cut down on paper and space.

- **It's up to you to market your rental property**
  - After you've scoped out a property and made the purchase, create a simple marketing plan for advertising your property to potential renters. This is the key to producing a self-sustaining cash flow: always have a renter or a renter lined up for a property. Advertising online is very effective and is a great way to get your opportunity out to large numbers of people for free or for cheap. More tenant applications will lead you to a greater applicant pool and allow you to choose the most desirable tenant based on income and rental history.

- **Ultimately you are in charge of your rental property portfolio**
  - In the end, you make the final decisions regarding how many properties to purchase, how much to spend on each for purchasing and maintenance and deciding on when to sell if that's what you want to do, and whether to pocket that money or turn around and reinvest it into another rental property. Only you, and your spouse if you have one, know what's right for your family and future.

Homeownership rates have fallen back to levels there were at around 1990, so if you have the money or the credit, now is a great time to start investing in rental property! Not only can you provide a housing option for someone in need but building up your own equity and wealth while doing so is a win-win situation.

Consider if all of the benefits listed above are worth the amount of work you will need to put into the property. Make sure that the property you purchase falls in line with your financial goals- you can be active or passive with the role you play in your investment and how much risk you are willing to take with that property. Maybe you are wondering if stocks and bonds would be a better and easier option for investing, but in the end, it all comes down to you- your personality, preferences, and management style.

Real estate is much more of a comfortable investment for the middle class; with real estate, you also manage your own investment, versus trusting management and auditors with stocks who may seek to defraud you. While this book is not about land investment, vacant land can produce serious cash flow and is a fantastic investment because of its low maintenance nature and versatility potential.

Another great purchase potential is foreclosed homes. When someone takes out a mortgage on a property they are promising to pay back the loan to the lender and it's quantified in a promissory note. If the borrower cannot make the payments, the lender can take possession of the house and sell it get back as much of their loan money as they can.

Seeing a return on your investment

If you take the plunge and purchase property, you want to make sure that the income you are receiving is making your investment worth it. Here are some tips to make sure you see the maximum return on your investment:

- Increasing your income
  - Coin operated laundry
  - Vending machines
  - Build a storage facility on the property
- Decreasing your expenses

- Have tenants pay for their own utilities
- Pay utilities for your tenants and include a fee for it in their monthly rent
- If you use a property manager, negotiate with them if you have more than one property to see if you can get a lower rate
- Focus on retaining great tenants
- Leveraging your property
    - When you refinance money out of the property you can leverage the money to put it into a new property

Chapter 2: How to Buy a Rental Property

Photo by Tom Thain on Unsplash

If after considering all the pros and cons you have decided to purchase a rental property, congratulations! The next step is scoping out the right property for you. A good rule of thumb is to start locally when purchasing a rental property. Don't worry so much as to purchasing local so you can act like a hawk over the property and constantly check on it. The important aspect is to buy a quality home, not necessarily a home that is close to you.

Conduct your research

Research market conditions in your area, desirable neighborhoods, and what a fair market price is for homes that could be great rental properties. Ask yourself, 'why should I get this home'? Starting in an area or neighborhood that you are familiar with is a good strategy for your first property. If you don't want to buy locally in an area you know personally, drive around the zip codes where you want to potentially purchase in and talk to neighbors and shop owners about their thoughts on the area. See if you can find out local development plans too- this will tell you if people and business are planning on moving into town or out of town to give you a better feel for the current and future market potential of the proposed home. The type of home you purchase, where the home is located, and what the neighborhood makeup is can greatly affect who your renters will be and what they value.

Other elements that can make the difference between a profitable house and a money pitfall are its location in relation to major roads, lines of public transportation, and school districts. Great properties that are always in high demand are single-family homes and apartment complexes, particularly in large urban areas or in smaller college towns. You should start small with your very first property though: if things don't work out as planned and you become unable to afford the home's mortgage or maintenance costs, you run a much less risk of going bankrupt. Try to stay away from homes needing significant repairs as your first few homes as well: taking on too much or at least more than you budgeted for in repairs can cause you to overextend your time and finances.

Homes in nicer neighborhoods will cost more to purchase up front but will have a bigger payoff for you down the road because the homes can be rented out at higher rates; homes in less desirable or dilapidated neighborhoods show lower income earnings and either an inability to make improvements or the homeowner does not care enough about the property to make it look nice. These neighborhoods will have a higher tenant turnover and probably less desirable tenants applying to live on your property.

Make sure the numbers add up and that the home will be worth your investment in time and money. Talk to other investors and get advice from people who have already purchased properties and are renting them out- many people are more than willing to let you in on insider tricks of the trade that they have learned over their many years of buying, selling, and managing properties. You'll want your rental properties to have anywhere from an 8-15% rate of return. Do your own research by conducting a sales comparison by finding out what properties have recently sold in the area similar to the home you are considering and match up your properties to others similar in size and amenities to determine how much the property is worth, its value, and its growth potential.

If you decide you don't want to necessarily stay local, consider purchasing all your properties in at least the same state. There are so many inefficiencies in having properties spanning several states due to different laws regarding taxes, having to have more than one property manager, and farther trips for checking in on your rentals. Don't try to spread yourself too thin. Bundle your properties into one, maybe two markets in order to be efficient, save time, and save money.

Pay attention to the condition of the house

As mentioned earlier, don't choose an obvious fixer-upper as your first rental property investment. You don't want to spend too much money on upgrading a property, especially your first one when you aren't sure yet if owning rentals are right for you, or if your plan hits a snag. For your first home, we highly suggest you hire a qualified professional to inspect the home and get quotes from contractors for any major jobs that would need to be completed.

Look to purchase a house that has good bones meaning it has quality construction, a solid infrastructure, good floor plan, spacious rooms, and character and natural light. When deciding if a house is right to purchase as your rental property, check for the following:

- **Quality of home construction**
  Do the floorboards bounce and creak as you walk through the house? Look at the doorways, joists, foundation wall, front porch if there is one and note the condition of the roofing as well. A good bet for quality materials includes stone and brick on the outside of the home and hardwood floors on the inside.

- **A solid infrastructure**
  It's relatively easy to replace plumbing and aging shingles, but if a quality foundation, heating, and electrical systems to name a few are already in good shape, potential renovations will become much easier. A solid roof and foundation are also important as they are some of the most expensive elements to fix or replace in a home.

- **Conducive floor plan**

Do you feel a good flow between frequently used rooms, and are the rooms placed in the most common sense way? Note the flow of traffic and whether the current set up is find the way it is or if you would need to do some renovations to fix that. Moving or taking out walls in a home can turn into a major project, so make sure you know what you are getting into with a property if you are willing to overlook the floor plan. The flow between rooms throughout a house can make or break interest in a home from a renting standpoint: it should be easy to get from one room to another, and related rooms should all be near each other.

- **Spacious rooms**
  Are the rooms in the home a useful size and shape? Are there enough rooms for the ideal family you would want to rent the home? Any older homes were much smaller than modern homes built to accommodate growing family sizes. Again, note your thoughts on the rooms and if you would need to make any adjustments to make the rooms more appealing or functional.

- **The character of the home and natural light usage**
  It's common for real estate developers to build all the homes in the same neighborhood in a similar fashion with only small differences between each home like trim finish or paint colors. While renters have fewer choices regarding what the outside of their dwelling looks like, homes that don't look too cookie cutter can be an advantage to drawing in renters. People also look for sunny, airy, and open home layouts for several reasons- natural light is a preference to artificial light and can lower electricity costs.

A home that has good bones *will* need some work, but the work should be cosmetic, not major repairs. Sometimes people will refer to a home with good bones as a less desirable property, more than likely due to its age, but good homes are the really the true foundation on which you can build a long-lasting and profitable rental property investment. Look into the property and see if it's zoned in a way that would prohibit you from expanding or converting the property into something else. You can also pull public permit records to see the last time a home had a new roof or a new furnace put in, for example, can help you negotiate during the negotiation process and lead to dollars saved in your pocket.

The buying process

Photo by rawpixel on Unsplash

Purchasing real estate can be complex and take a long time to complete the entire process; this section will briefly break down the steps from beginning to end to purchase a rental investment property:

1. Decide that you want to invest in rental property and plan out your investment strategy- both short and long-term
    o Property choices range from raw land to single-family homes, to duplexes, triplexes, and quads, to small and large apartment complexes, to real estate investment trusts (which we will cover later in this chapter), to commercial properties and mobile homes or mobile home parks. For the purpose of this book, we will not be discussing mobile homes, raw land, or commercial properties.

To produce wealth there are several common strategies to choose between that will help you make money including:

   o *Buy and hold onto the property*
   This strategy involves purchasing a property and renting it out over a long period of time. The homeowner earns money by collecting monthly rent from their tenant, or by holding onto the property and selling down the road when the real estate market is hot. You will also pay down the mortgage every month which will, over time, increase your own equity.

   o *Flip your property*
   Flipping homes is the process of purchasing a home at a discounted price, making improvements, and then selling it at a financial gain. Speed is the key because in order to receive maximum profitability and to avoid month-to-month carrying costs of the home.

- *Wholesale real estate*

  This process requires the purchaser to write a contract acquiring the home before then selling that contract off to another buyer. The wholesaler never actually owns the home- they simply find the best deal, contracting it, and selling the contract for a fee.

- *Commercial real estate*

  Purchase a commercial building and rent out the floors and spaces to different companies and organizations. You will have a higher income potential because commercial rentals produce more money than residential investments and you can charge more rent for businesses. Your relationship with the renters comes in a more professional capacity when you work in the commercial real estate because tenants work hard to make sure your property stays in tip-top shape and retains its value. The downside of this strategy is that it requires more capital up front which leads to a higher risk of costs outweighing capital gains.

- *Airbnb*

  This popular website allows hosts to list their properties as a short-term rental. These tenants are less likely to damage your property as they will only be there for a few nights or a few weeks. Rental rates per night or per week can have investors seeing greater gains than monthly rent from a steady tenant. Varying from city to city, short-term rentals have specific taxes that must be paid on them and other limits set by the city as to how many times a place can be rented out per year or how many people can occupy a property.

2. Define your home selection criteria

- Some criteria to start should be city, neighborhood, square footage of the property site and the size of the lot it's on, what the condition of the property is, appreciation potential, and what the cash flow will be to name a few. Being able to define what you are looking for will make your search for a property way more manageable, and it will make it easier to articulate your desires to a real estate agent or others who can help you purchase a property.

3. Determine how you will be financing the property
   - If you are planning on paying with all cash, you'll want to have that money available to liquidate and be used to purchase the home. If you will be financing the home with a bank loan, you'll want to get a pre-approval. The larger the down payment you can make up front, the less you will pay toward the total price of the property down the road.

4. Begin searching for properties to purchase
   - Start searching for properties on the multiple listing services (MLS), commercial sites, newspaper and website ads, yard signs, and other avenues used to advertise properties for sale. You can also search out a real estate agent at this point, and they are typically "free" for the buyer as they are paid out of the closing costs of selling the home. If you choose to not use an agent, you will probably be contacting the sellers directly themselves.

5. Quickly run each property through your list of criteria
   - Use the list you established earlier to screen out properties that don't meet your needs or standards.

6. Get pre-approved at the bank of your choice

- Shop around when comparing mortgage rates is that's how you plan on purchasing your home- not many of us have $250,000 cash to put down on a place. Sites like LendingTree can help you compare rates online so that the only other thing you have to do is choose the best offer and attempt to get the lowest interest rate the bank will give you.

7. Make an offer on the property you want to purchase
   - Offer less than you are willing to spend or start by offering your top price. An offer is typically made using a Purchase and Sale Agreement that your real estate agent will complete for you should you choose to use one. Otherwise, you can find a free fill-in-the-blank form from an attorney or from a local Title and Escrow company. We recommend that if you do not go through a real estate agent, have a real estate attorney review the agreement for you.

8. Negotiate and close the deal
   - If everything goes the way it is supposed to you should be able to negotiate a selling price and come to mutually accepted agreement terms.

9. Submit paperwork and prepare for closing
   - Inspect the property and provide the details over to a Title and Escrow company or a local real estate attorney. Submit paperwork to your chosen bank for financing, start to search for contractors if work will be needed, and prepare the close on the sale. This process can take time depending on the bank financing, so paying with all cash can make the closing process go faster.

10. Sign title papers
    - Sign the agreement at the Title and Escrow office or at your attorney's office. Once the

paperwork is recorded, the property is officially in your name as the new owner.

Generally speaking, the process is quite straightforward. To ensure the best outcome, stick to your bottom line regarding price and negotiations, and seek out help from a real estate agent or real estate attorney if this is your first time purchasing unless you are very confident in your own abilities. There's no harm in using professional help your first time around and then taking on those responsibilities yourself should you choose to pursue investing in real estate.

Will you hire a property manager or manage the property yourself?

If you only have one property at the moment, you may ask yourself if it's worth your money to hire a property manager. In real estate, the rule of thumb is that a property manager is completely necessary for five or more properties, although many people choose to go that route after three. If you choose to manage your own property, here are some tips and tricks:

- Establish proper processes like building reusable rental form templates
  - If you are tech savvy you can buy a landlord property management software to help you track payments, leases, and contractor contact information.
- Keep up with property maintenance by using a spreadsheet or another system that works for you to track how often you've inspected the property, issues you've discovered, how you've remedied them, and how much money you spent on the repairs.
- Going off of that necessary maintenance, have on hand at least 3 go-to contacts in the following areas:
  - Plumbing
  - Electricity

- HVAC
- Roofing and gutters
- Lawn care
- General Repairs
- Remodels
- Appliance repairs

Based on your own needs and expectations, hiring a property manager could be the best bet for running your rental property efficiently, especially if you have a separate full-time job. If the property you purchased is not in your area, finding a local property manager can reduce your stress associated with being a long-distance landlord so working with someone who knows local service providers can be a life-saver in an emergency. To go about finding a great property manager follow these steps:

- Research local property managers and ask them for an estimate to make sure the numbers work
- Get recommendations from family, friends, and colleagues for property managers they have worked with in the past; another place to try is your local apartment association.
- Make sure that the manager you hire is familiar with your own personal standards and the laws they must adhere to regarding the Fair Housing Act; many property management contracts have what is called a 'hold harmless' clause which means you can be held liable for their actions except in cases of gross negligence.
- Ask the potential property manager the following questions to make sure that who you hire falls in line with your core values:

  - What services do you offer?
  - How many units are you currently managing?
  - Do you set your own rent prices?
  - Are you a real estate investor?
  - How much do you charge?

- How is rent collected?
- Do you have a marketing plan for any of your properties?
- What are your vacancy rates?
- Are you a more hands-on or passive property manager?

Hiring a property manager to handle the direct, day-to-day interactions on your behalf with applicants and tenants can really lighten up your workload and responsibilities. These managers will usually handle the marketing and advertising of your rental, handle property showings, collect rent payments and deposits into your bank account, and coordinate maintenance repairs.

Excellent property managers should have open and regular communication with the property owner. Their main job is to oversee your investment and ensure that the property is being taken care of with little to no oversight from you.

Are you worried about being able to afford a property manager if you feel like managing your own property is not right for you? Property management costs can have a large range depending on the scope of the engagement,

A typical fee agreement between a landlord and property manager can cost anywhere from 8-12% of the monthly rental value of the property, sometimes plus the cost of expenses. Some companies may just charge a flat rate- depending on your monthly rental rate that could be more or less than the 8-12% of rental payment so make the arrangement that will end up saving you the most money. These other potential fees include, but are not limited to the following:

- A vacant unit
  - Some managers or management firms charge upfront the cost of one month's rent; engage the manager while the property has tenants in order to avoid this fee. This fee would provide cash to the property manager to pay a real estate agent commission for finding a renter for the property

or to pay for advertising, showing the property, or preparing lease paperwork.
- Placing a new tenant
  - A fee of up to 50% of a month's worth of rent for a new tenant placed is not unusual- a property manager will normally require this and an upfront fee or first-month rental fee.
- Maintenance
  - This is not likely a fee you will run into working with an individual property manager, but some property management companies have their own full-time maintenance crew. Ask the company what routine maintenance services are included as part of your contract, and don't be afraid to negotiate to get the specific services you need and not have to pay for services you don't want or can't use. Make sure that your contract states the terms of how much the company can charge you.
- Evictions
  - Sometimes tenants don't work out for a whole slew of reasons, and many property managers will charge you a fee to go through the eviction process which can cost anywhere from $250-500 per eviction plus any court costs that may accrue.
- Collecting late payments

If you find an individual or a company that you think would be a great property manager for your investment rental, make sure you read through the details and stipulations of the contract you would be entering with them. Terminology and language are important, and ultimately you and this person or company will be partners in managing your property.

Creating a fool-proof strategy for investing

In order to ensure that the property you buy will produce income, these strategies are fool-proof for ensuring a solid investment:

1. Buy properties that are 10-20% under market value
    To afford your financial security, that 10-20% will allow you to sell the home faster should an emergency happen or the market crashes.

2. Calculate the numbers to ensure the property will generate at a minimum a 15% return on investment (ROI)
    If you take the monthly rent and subtract the debt of the home (a mortgage if there is one) and its monthly expenses you can find your cash flow. Instead of guessing to determine how much your investment is worth, calculate it yourself or use an online tool that will take into account the following: expected rental income, repairs and maintenance, property management fees, insurance, property taxes, advertising or marketing, utilities, mortgage payment, vacancy, and HOA fees if applicable.

3. Buy a property in a 'B Class' neighborhood where there are about 35% renters
    These neighborhoods have a wide range of homes that typically serve a large number of people in a community and have a large inventory of homes available. Blue collar workers are stable homeowners and can provide a great neighborhood framework for a little over that 1/3 mix of renters to homeowners that you want to look for.

4. Set the rent price as 1% of the purchase price of the home minimum
    For example, a home that cost you $150,000 should rent for at least $1,500 a month.

Some of us thrive on writing down goals, outlining steps, or long-term strategizing for success. Create a real estate investing plan to guide you in the right direction while also keeping you motivated. Items you should think about including in your plan:

- A mission statement
  What is the purpose of buying a rental property? What benefits will this property provide you? A mission statement is a 'why' statement- the reason behind the actions.

- Your goals
  What are you hoping owning rental property will help you achieve? How much money do you want to bring in monthly? Yearly? Goals change over time so being flexible and breaking down your goals over time will help you achieve momentum and deal with less stress. Setting short, medium, and long-term goals will help you stay looking forward and celebrating victories along the way.

- Desired time frame
  When do you want to reach your goals? Outlining a time frame will allow you to set a pact and work hard to achieve your goals by your deadline.

- Markets you are interested in
  Where are you interested in purchasing a property? Do you want a home in an urban or suburban location? As a beginner, we suggest purchasing in an area you are familiar with and is within a short distance from your current home.

- Strategize
  Maybe you plan to live in each of your rental properties for a year or two before renting them out. Determine the strategy you want to pursue while investing and stick to it even if deals come your way that doesn't meet your needs.

- Set criteria
  Before you even begin searching for properties to purchase, write down the criteria a home must meet in order for you to purchase it. Maybe that criteria is how much cash flow you want to see every month, a price range target, the number of bedrooms, etc. Even if you come across a great deal if one or more of your criteria are missing you can easily turn the property down if it is not up to your standards.

- Create a marketing plan
  Lead generation is important, so establishing a system to continuously bring potential tenants to your property will cut down on the time and money you have to spend searching for tenants and telling people you have a vacant property.

- Financing

What money will you use to purchase the home? Do you have your own money or will you need to take out a loan? There is a wide range of funding options, so make sure you do your research and choose the best option for you and your financial situation.

- Acquisition
  What will you do after the home is purchased? Will you take it upon yourself to manage the property, or will you hire a property manager?

- Systems
  Define your team, and the kinds of systems you will need to have in place to automate and delegate tasks.

- Exit strategy and a backup plan
  A strong plan will include multiple exit strategies: what will you do if you decide you won't want to go through with the deal? What is your backup plan in case the deal falls through or your property doesn't earn you enough money or any money?

- Example deals
  This is where you can get creative and have some fun! In this section of the plan you can illustrate your desired purchases, cash flow projections, and to see where your path could take you on the way to reaching your goals.

- Snapshot of current financials
  What can you contribute to the investment property and where do you fall short? Do you have a steady income to support yourself or equity in your current home you can use? What is your current net worth? Map out what your current cost of living is and re-evaluate your financial situation at least twice a year.

Should you invest in a real estate investment trust (REIT) instead of purchasing an investment property?

A REIT is a company that owns, operates, or finances real estate that produces an income. Based on mutual fund models, these trusts provide an investor with the chance to own real estate, access dividends and returns, and help communities expand and thrive. Stockholders earn a share of the income produced through real estate investments without having to spend their own time and money on buying, financing, or managing their own property. There are 4 different kinds of REITs:

1. Equity
   Most REITs are publicly traded, but Equity REITs own or operate income-generating real estate.

2. Mortgage
   These REITs provide financing for income-generating real estate through the purchasing of mortgages and mortgage-backed securities that earn an income from the investment interest.

3. Public non-listed
   Listed with the SEC, these REITs do not trade on a national stock exchange market.

4. Private
   Exempt from SEC registration, these types of Private REITs also do not trade on the stock exchange.

Investors earn money from REITs in the form of dividends as the REIT pays out of its taxable income. REITs are defined legally as the following:

- Invest at minimum 75% of its total assets into real estate

- Earn at least 75% of its gross income from rental property rents, interest on mortgage financing, or from the sale of real estate
- Shareholder dividends should make up at least 90% of its taxable income to be paid out
- Entity that is taxable as a corporation
- Managed by a board of directors or trustees
- Shareholders must be no less than 100 people, and no more than 50% of its shares can be held by 5 or fewer individuals

What are the benefits of investing in a REIT? Historically they have delivered competitive returns and can act as a great portfolio diversifier to reduce portfolio risk and increase your chance of returns. Similar to other stocks and investing options, a REIT can provide you with long-term, stable returns that continue providing a profit despite a variety of market conditions.

REITs are also monitored by independent directors, analysts, and auditors to keep track of the REIT's performance and projected outlook. This provides investors with more protection because your investment is being watched by several outside sources who also have their interests in the REIT. According to Reit.com, "more than 80 million Americans are invested in REITs directly or through REIT mutual funds or exchange-traded funds (ETFs). In addition, institutional investors like pension funds, endowments, foundations, insurance companies and bank trust departments invest in REITs."

A REIT isn't the only way to go: other online platforms have emerged that have made real estate investments easier, cheaper, and provide higher returns to investors. A great site to start on is Fundrise who offers a diversified commercial real estate platform online with low fees and it's available to anyone living in the United States.

Is purchasing a rental home right for you?

If after doing your research, crunching the numbers, and speaking to others in the field, you decide that investing in rental property is right for you- congratulations! You can choose to manage your own property, hire a property manager, and oversee the financials to ensure your property is being kept up-to-date. After purchasing your first property, the next step may be to begin scoping out other purchase opportunities to increase and grow your portfolio and earning potential.

Photo by Brina Blum on Unsplash

How to decide what kind of rental property will work best for you

Traditionally single-family homes don't depreciate as much, and there are more opportunities to expand the home vs buying an apartment complex, condo, or co-op. If you have no family or a small family, a good bet would be to invest in a multi-unit property to see the greatest financial returns. Owning many smaller units will earn you more money than say, owning three or four bedroom units. A one-bedroom that rents out for $2,000 a month will give you more earning power than a two-bedroom that rents for $2,700. A four bed won't rent for $4,000 a month so why not save yourself some work and focus on smaller units. If you would rather save your money and not hire a property manager, a single-family home will be the best buy; you can even live in one of your units while you rent the others out will likely maximize your return, and tenants will probably treat the property better than usual because they know you are living there as well.

Investing to give yourself a better lifestyle should be first on your list, followed by the need or want to earn rental income, followed lastly by what you want your overall capital appreciation will be. Enjoying your money is much better than trying to turn that money into more money- why not just enjoy what you already have? Properties can be held onto for a long time where you can look to receive small, stable payments over time, or properties can be purchased and sold in a quick turnaround time to make a little bit of money.

Funding sources for purchasing an investment rental property

Line up your financing *before* you go to find a great deal. Money lenders come in many forms, and we will outline them below for you to choose the lender that best fits your needs:

- Private money lenders
  An individual lends you their own capital to an investor or professionally managed fund while securing that loan with a mortgage against a real estate asset. Their presence makes it much more accessible for the average property investor to run and maintain a long-lasting career. These investors are best for short-term fixer uppers and flips that want to quickly purchase, renovate and sell a property quickly as well as those who want to do more extensive rehabilitation. Private money lenders are also referred to as hard money lenders who have terms lasting usually around 1 year (but can go anywhere from 2-5 years) and they require that interest and some principal payments be made on the loan each month. Lenders are more concerned with the property value rather than the borrower's credit score.

- Traditional lenders
  A traditional lender would be a bank or credit union that can issue a long-term loan to finance a real estate purchase. Using this type of lender will require you to have a stable income and a good credit score, and it will require you to put 10-20% down on the purchase of a home's total value. You can put down less than 10%, but when that happens you will be required to pay a mortgage insurance rate until your equity hits at least at that 10% mark. The process of using a traditional lender will require a lot of critique from the bank regarding your financial profile, and it may take anywhere from several weeks to several months to close on the loan application.

Understand the difference between a Realtor and a real estate agent

These terms are often used interchangeably when in fact there are key differences between the two, hence the two separate terms. A real estate agent is a licensed sales professional that can help you buy, sell, or rent a property. They are qualified to handle all of the documents in a real estate transaction and mediate between a buyer and a seller during purchase negotiations. A real estate agent has taken real estate courses, passed a licensing exam, and maintained their license and kept it current with education requirements.

A Realtor is a real estate professional that is also a member of the National Association of Realtors (NAR). A real estate agent can also be a Realtor but they will have access to the local boar's MLS and keybox systems, are involved in the industry and laws that govern them and abide by a Realtor Code of Ethics. To receive this qualification a person must be a real estate professional, pay membership dues to NAR, and uphold that code of ethics. They are also governed by 17 principles that include but are not limited to prioritizing client interests, non-discrimination, the disclosure of conflicts of interest, and providing clear written documents for their clients.

Chapter 3: Owning a Rental Property

Photo by Gus Ruballo on Unsplash

Now that you've decided that you want to dip your toe into investing in rental properties, you will have to set yourself up for success to oversee your property, or your property manager if you have one, and continually run the numbers to ensure that your properties are earning you money and not running you into a hole.

Organization is key to lasting success

Focus on task management, not time management. Set goals, make to-do lists, and keep detailed records. Start these records by logging incoming and outgoing phone calls you make in a centralized location to hold all of your contacts and conversations- this will come as a big help to keep information on hand while you have a conversation. As a real estate investor and landlord, you will be responsible for making mortgage payments, paying property taxes, and maintaining your property to name a few. You keep your own financial records, and when you decide to purchase rental property store all of the paperwork you have collected since the purchase of the home in one place for current and future reference.

Instead of a folder for each property, another good idea is to keep a binder for each investment property you own. Take a photo of the property, print it out, and put it on the front cover of the binder to help you remember which property you are dealing with. Tabs inside your binder can include paperwork for the house like the purchase contract, other photos of the inside and outside of the home when you first purchased it and then maybe between tenants as well to document the maintenance you have done or the damage the tenants have caused. This can also be a place to store contact information for companies or individual handymen to call on in case something in your property breaks. This binder should also hold property management statements if there are any, invoices and receipts, bank statements, and property tax receipts.

Use technology to your benefit

Most of us rely on accessibility to technology to keep up to date and organized. If for some reason your cell phone breaks, a hack is to keep a digital camera stored in your car. If you plan on stopping by your property and end up needing to take photos, a digital camera can save the day and even make your life easier by allowing you to sync or store all your photos on a designated place on your computer.

Learning how to leverage technology will allow you to lighten your workload and can be used to find resources for general investing knowledge, viewing listings, finding assessors and legal forms, and performing credit checks. Many sites now have mobile apps that allow even easier accessibility.

Developing a filing system can help eliminate excessive paperwork that can end up being distracting and time-consuming. Try to tackle paperwork as you receive it based on each property you own. Each property can have a different file for applications, leases, and any other information pertaining to the property. A website like Shoebox or Google Dropbox can be a place to scan and store receipts and conduct online banking. If you've got the money, software like Quicken can automate your paperwork, or pay for an online rent payment system like eRentPayment will make it easier for tenants to pay you and make it easier to see and generate reports concerning financial statements and bill payments.

Implement plans to deal with complaints, maintenance requests, and move-outs

As a landlord, you will deal with property emergencies like leaky pipes, broken windows, and an A/C unit that quits during a midsummer heat wave. Document that you received the request in your call/interaction log and strive to address issues quickly to keep tenants happy and stop small problems from spiraling into big, expensive issues. Many problems can be prevented by performing regular maintenance, and you should consider implementing a schedule for your properties to keep up with wear-and-tear.

Laying out policies and procedures to give out with the lease outlining the notice tenants are required to give, what condition you expect the property to be in when the tenant moves out, what your steps for property inspection will be, and how you will return the security deposit.

Crunch the numbers to see if your property has long-term potential

Figure out the overall picture of your property's income by calculating the gross rent multiplier (GRM), the 1% rule, cap rate, net income after financing, and the property's cash on cash return. The next step is to estimate the current value of the property or the value after repairs, followed by a calculation of the property equity. How to calculate:

1. GRM

To find the gross rent multiplier you take the total rent before subtracting expenses or any other deductions. To calculate, take the total purchase price and divide it by the yearly gross rent. This number will give you an idea of how good your property is at producing you a profit. The higher the GRM, the less likely an investment rental property will be at giving you your desired income.

2. 1% rule
While the GRM focuses more on yearly rent, following the 1% rule focuses more on monthly rent figures. This statement says that the gross rent of your investment property should equal, at minimum, 1% of the property purchase price.

3. Cap rate
A cap rate can give a great number that will lead you as the owner to understand how much income your property is producing after expenses. To calculate this number, take your net operating income (which does not include financing costs) and divide it by the total purchase price to find your cap rate. Some investors use this rate as a minimum investment goal, meaning that this rate is set as an acceptable investment for said property.

4. Net income after financing
Your net operating income assumes that 50% of your gross rent will be lost to your operating expenses but you'll also want to see how much income is left over after you deduct your financing costs for the home. Before tax, you can calculate the net income by taking your net operating income minus financing costs.

5. Cash on cash return

This calculation will tell you how much of your down payment or cash investment will come back to you in the form of cash each year. To calculate this number take the net income after financing costs and divide it by the down payment or total cash you invested. Cash flow is important to surviving long-term as a real estate investor

Find a property manager that's a good fit for you

Make sure that you and your property manager are on the same page from the get-go. Open and frequent communication with the individual or company you choose to work with should be established when you decide to start working together. Let the property manager know how often you want to hear from them with updates and questions and make it a regular occurrence.

As mentioned in previous chapters, find a quality property manager by doing your research: look online, ask for references from friends and family, and have some questions prepared. Even if you decide to outsource your work to a property manager, continue to keep and store your own records for back up and just to ensure all the numbers add up.

When you run the numbers, include the price of a property manager if that's the way you are looking to go. Many companies charge monthly fees, but you can also find property managers that cater their services to only the ones you need- paying for services you don't need or can't use is a waste of your hard-earned money.

Continue to handle the tasks you enjoy or would prefer to handle yourself like collecting rent and let your property manager know which tasks you want them to take over from you like scheduling maintenance or showing and renting your property.

Renting out your property

Photo by Mike Marquez on Unsplash

Should you decide to handle the renting out of the property instead of having your property manager do that, create procedures to ensure all potential tenants have a fair and equal chance to rent the property. This year marks the 50th anniversary of the Fair Housing Act, so it's important to make sure no one can come back and question how you screened potential tenant 'A' for your rental but turned down potential tenant 'B'. It's illegal to discriminate against potential tenants based on the 7 protected classes as outlined in the Fair Housing Act. Make sure that in your screening, advertising, and renting processes everyone is treated equally and you won't have any problems.

Create a reusable template for applications and save printed copies in your filing cabinets and electronically. Keep printed copies on hand in a folder to give out to interested parties, and another place to keep the returned forms. You'll have to pay a company to run credit checks for you and maybe another to verify income, but either way, once you receive an approval or a denial for an applicant make sure the ruling is documented as to why a party was not allowed to live in your rental property.

Create a lease that outlines the policies of tenancy, and have it looked over by a real estate lawyer to ensure compliance and legality. Make sure that your tenants understand the terms of the lease before agreeing to sign it- there's nothing worse than something happening and a tenant claiming they were not aware of the terms stated in the lease. Again, store several copies of this lease in several different forms (hard copy and electronic), and it also wouldn't be bad to sit down with your tenants when you hand over the keys to go over policies you want to make sure they remember; for example, you want to remind them that no smoking is allowed inside the property and that you also do not allow pets other than service animals. Reiterate the monthly date that you want rent paid by, and what the fees and penalties will be for paying rent late; one way to make it easier for both of you is to allow for payment of rent online!

Outline the procedures for maintenance requests and let them know what your procedure will be for handling these requests and how they can coordinate with you to ensure work gets completed. This can be a conversation to lay a solid foundation for a great relationship with your tenant- lay down your boundaries and learn what your tenant wants from you to ensure they are satisfied with your property.

A step by step process to renting out your property

After you sign the papers and closing and the property turns over into your hands, the first step should be to make any necessary repairs or small renovations that need to be done before you can move in your first tenants. Until you get your first tenant in, all of the money you are spending on fixing up the property will be coming out of your own pocket.

The next step should be to start advertising your property- you can't rent it out if no one knows that it's there and available to them. Start by taking clear and crisp quality photos of the inside and outside of the property. You can list the property using a realtor or go about listing it on your own on websites such as Craigslist, Zillow, Trulia, Rent.com, and by placing signage in the yard. There are many other ways to advertise- these are just a few ideas to get you started. Once you've begun advertising, you will begin to receive interest in the property via calls from potential tenants.

If you listed the property without using a real estate agent, it will be your responsibility to meet these prospective tenants at the property and show it to them yourself. Make sure your property looks nice and clean and try to schedule showings back to back or within the same day or time period to save time and travel to and from the property.

Running your property without a property manager will require you to handle applications and credit checks as well. As mentioned earlier, using a standard application template that you created will streamline the application process, and ensure you are giving everyone who applies a fair chance at qualifying for your property. Make sure you screen potential tenants thoroughly by contacting previous landlords, current job supervisors, public records, etc. to give you a better picture of the person you will be renting to.

Once you choose a tenant that meets your requirements and whom you think will be a good fit, you will need to ratify your lease. We'll give you some tips later on in the chapter about what to include in your lease and other items we suggest you include. Meet with the tenant and go over the lease making sure to highlight important aspects, and then both of you will sign it to indicate that you have entered into an agreement together. Collect the security deposit before the tenant moves in (also a last month's rent deposit or pet deposit if applicable).

Complete a walk-thru of the property with the tenant to make sure there are no issues or areas of concern before you hand over the keys to their new rental property. Make sure they know when you expect rent to be paid every month and how they can send that payment to you.

Writing a lease

A lease is another great example of when using a template will save you time and money. You would rather be safe than sorry when it comes to specifics, so make sure you include everything. Legal Zoom is a great site where you can purchase a local real estate lease form that you can then add to and alter based on new information. A great tip is to keep the lease blank, write down your own answers to the blanks, then go over the lease with your new tenant and have them fill in the blanks themselves- you have the paper to reference with your own answers if you blank while going through the form. If you include any addendums to the lease have the tenant initial the lease next to each one to cover your bases.

Photo by Andrew Neel on Unsplash

Useful addendums:
- Automatic lease renewal

A standard lease runs for 12 months, but many landlords choose to extend the terms after the lease is over by switching to a month-to-month lease. Some landlords charge a fee the renew to the month-to-month option, meaning from then on a tenant only has to give you 30 days' notice to leave with no consequences.

- Late fees
Charge 10% of the monthly rent if you receive rent late. Include a 5 day grace period but charge the fee on the 6th.

- Pet fees
We all love our furry friends, but sometimes bad owners let their pets wreak havoc on a property. Decide if you want to charge a monthly pet fee or a pet deposit. Include the pet's name and age and have the tenant write these details down on the lease for you. This information prevents your tenant from taking in more pets than they are allowed to have on the property as per stated in the lease.

- Utilities
Some landlords make it easier and just pay for the property's utilities, and others may choose to have the tenant incur all the fees, sometimes including landscaping

- Smoking
Let tenants know that they are not allowed to smoke while inside the property and warn them that if you discover smoking damage they will be fined up to $500.

- Maintenance
Outline the work you will pay for that must be authorized with your writing and signature. You may also want to require that your tenants assume routine maintenance fees associated with certain appliances, yard maintenance, smoke detectors, carbon monoxide detectors, etc.

- Lease termination

Unless a tenant is military personnel and can provide you with their orders, charge a fee for lease termination under circumstances where tenants give less than 30 days' notice or move out before their original 12-month lease ends.

- Cleaning
  You can choose to require your tenant to professionally steam clean the carpet upon moving out and require that the tenant return the house to the state that it looks professionally cleaned. If you as the landlord determine that the property has not been cleaned properly and you must hire someone to clean it, you can reserve the right to keep a portion of a tenant's security deposit.

- Landscaping
  In an apartment complex it's common for the landlord to pay the landscaping fees, but in a single-family home, you can hold the tenant responsible for the lawn and general yard maintenance. If your home is located in a homeowners association (HOA), the tenants will be required to abide by the HOA rules as well. Hold the tenants responsible for any landscaping that deteriorates due to neglect or mismanagement.

- Fines
  If you determine the tenant has incurred fines make sure they notice in the lease that they need to pay fines immediately and that if they still have fines by the time move out day comes around those fines will be deducted from their security deposit.

- Keys and remotes

In case keys or remotes are lost, stolen, broken, or damaged in any way by a tenant or their guest the tenant is responsible for the costs to replace said items, as well as pay for the cost of a locksmith if needed. If the locks on the home need to be changed at any time, ask the tenant that they let you know so you can change the locks yourself but at their expense. Let the tenant know that you will have a key to the property at all times, but that as per the lease terms you will never enter the property without 48 hours warning in written notice.

- Damages
  Damages will be assessed upon tenant moving out, and as stated before, will be taken out of the tenant's security deposit.
- Renter's insurance
  Require that tenants get renter's insurance upon moving into the property in an amount that can cover their personal property items and liability. Point out in the lease that you will assume no responsibility for tenant's or guest's property.
- Buyout
  This option in the lease addendum allows the tenant or you as the landlord to break the lease without penalty, provided 60 days' notice and upon paying a breaking lease fee. The tenant will be given a fee if they move out before the 60 days.

Items to replace or upgrade frequently

Frequently upgrading the following items can make your rental property rental rates go higher and doing preventative work will usually end up saving you money down the road.

1. Toilet

When toilets start to leak your water bill will continue to grow and grow, especially if the leak goes undetected for an amount of time. These can leak all day every day, whereas a leaky faucet would only run up a very small fraction of a toilet water bill. This kind of repair is only needed on the inside of the toilet, although between long-term tenants it's not a bad idea to replace the toilet in general.

2. Locks

   Whether you allow the tenants to change your own locks or reserve the right to change the locks for the tenants, this should always be done between tenants because you never know who has a key. You can save money by recycling locks between properties if you own multiple.

3. Lights

   Common areas in the home should have long lasting, energy saving light bulbs to reduce the overall electricity bill.

4. Outlets

   Think about upgrading to special GFCI electric outlets that can shut off automatically if they detect that electricity is running through an unintended path. These outlets are more expensive but may be required by law in certain states for safety reasons if placing outlets near kitchen countertops, sinks, or the washer and dryer.

5. Fire extinguishers and smoke alarms

   If you have been keeping track of how often the smoke alarms and fire extinguishers have been checked and replaced if needed, err on the side of caution and change them between tenants,

Legal landlord responsibilities

There are many legal implications of being a landlord, and if you fail to comply with the rules you may be fined heavily. Your responsibilities start with the tenant's security deposit that they pay over to you: not all states go as in depth-describing how you must hold their funds, it's always smart not to co-mingle your personal finances with your rental finances. You must repay the tenant their security deposit at the end of their tenancy unless you require that the pay damages. Never spend the deposit and plan on paying the money back when the time comes that it's due!

Even though you own the property, now that the tenants are renting it from you it is the tenant's home, and they have the right to live there without being disturbed by you. If you need access to the property for repairs or any other reason, you must give the tenants notice a suitable amount of time in advance, at least 24-48 hours. Again, despite owning the property, while it is being rented out you cannot enter the property without the tenant's consent. Since you will be required to keep up with most of the repairs of the property, including the exterior and structure, you must also make sure the maintenance of the equipment that supplies the water, gas, and electricity to the house is in a safe and working order.

Be very clear and upfront with your tenants when it comes to paying rent. Let them know how much is due, when it is due, and how you want them to pay. You cannot increase the rent whenever you feel like it- there are only certain circumstances during a tenancy that will allow you to increase the rent. Generally speaking, a landlord cannot change any aspect of the lease during the stated lease term unless the change is made upon mutual agreement.

You must provide your tenants with your contact information including your name, address, and phone number- or if you are using a property manager give them their contact information as well.

If you end up needed to evict a tenant or regain possession of your property for some other reason for the terms of the lease are over, you must have sufficient grounds to do so. A Section 8 Notice must be served, or you may have to go to court and get an order for possession if necessary. You can't just take the property back from the tenants; if you fail to follow the proper legal process the tenant can have a good case against you in court.

Getting into out of state real estate investing

Diversifying is a great idea, and as you deal in real estate you may decide that you want to expand your purchase borders outside of your own city or even state, and that can easily be achieved with a little extra flexibility. This process will be greatly eased if you have a local contact where you are looking to buy. They can give you the inside scoop on the area, hook you up with local real estate agents, and if you end up buying a property they may even agree to keep an eye on it for you until you either move in yourself or can get your very first tenants in.

When looking out of state for property one of the best times to buy is in the winter, sellers are typically more likely to negotiate to sell their home quickly. The other great thing about acquiring property in the winter means you can use those months for repairs and have the place all fresh and new for tenants in the spring months.

Instead of trusting your local contact for insight, it is important and one point or another to check out the neighborhood with your own eyes. See if the property is near any great amenities like local shops, schools, or lines of transportation. We've talked a lot throughout the book about hiring a property manager, but this the only time we will recommend that you invest in one- when you purchase out of state property. If you don't you will have to travel back and forth between your properties to deal with tenants and repairs.

Lastly, learn about the local state laws regarding rental properties. Each state can vary drastically about what you can and can't do as a landlord and things you must do. Different places require different documentation, so finding a local property manager or realtor can help make sure you stay protected. Some states are considered tenant-friendly, such as D.C., and others are landlord-friendly like Maryland. States that favor a tenant's rights when disputes arise can make it difficult to handle certain situations like unpaid rent in the winter.

Chapter 4: Potential Rental Property Pit Falls

Photo by rawpixel on Unsplash

When purchased and managed the right way, and investment rental property can earn the investor a great return on their investment, but we all know life doesn't always work out the way we planned. In order to best assess if owning rental property is right for you, take into consideration the fact that the following bad things could happen:

- High property taxes
  - While owners of rental properties receive preferential tax breaks from the government, you will still have to pay a property tax. Now is a great time to hire an accountant or bookkeeper, especially if you are considering purchasing additional investment rental properties. You will be paying taxes on the current property you own and live in on top of taxes for your rental property. Some landlords include a small portion

of that cost in the amount of rent they charge their tenant to help offset some of the costs.

- More damage by tenants then normal wear and tear
  - A property wears down over time as does everything else, but if you get tenants that are rougher on your property you will end up spending a lot of money repairing the damage the tenant caused. One of the only determinants of whether a tenant will be rough on a property is to speak to past landlords about the condition that tenant left their property in. Try to not judge people based on appearances as to whether they will treat your property nicely- looks can be deceiving.
- General repair costs
  - Normal wear and tear from people living in a home are bound to occur, but as the landlord, you are expected to keep the property at a certain standard, and constantly repairing things to keep up can be costly as well. Walls will need to be painted between tenants, but large unforeseen repairs can take a chunk out of your savings so having a cash cushion will stop you from having to take out money from your personal accounts. You can save yourself money by purchasing a home warranty that goes for around $500 a year- tell your tenant up-front that every time they directly contact the warranty company about a repair they will need to pay a deductible. Having this set up will drastically reduce your maintenance and associated costs.
- Property sits empty for more than a month between tenants
  - Hopefully, you've been putting other money inside in case you can't get the property rented. Research what the average vacancy rate in your property's area, but a good rule of thumb is to assume that your investment rental property will sit empty for about a month each year. Empty property can also pose a security risk if sitting

vacant for a period of time. Be wary of how long you leave a 'for rent' sign in the yard, let neighbors know that the property is vacant and see if they can keep an eye on it for you, visit frequently turn on different lights in the home.

- Legal expenses if tenants take you to court
  - If a tenant refuses to pay their rent on time or stops paying altogether, you will need to take them to court to get them evicted from your property and to collect the rent you are due. You will have to pay for these expenses out of pocket so you may end up spending more on the legal process than getting paid late rent you are due.
- The market crashes or you bought a house in a declining city
  - Maybe you thought you did a great job researching the housing market in the area you purchased your investment rental property, but over the years your property either loses its value or the housing market crashes and now you own a home worth much less than you purchased it for. Residential resident properties are a better bet, but you will most likely see more yields from a commercial investment property.

As mentioned earlier, real estate investing is not for everyone, and if you fit into any of the following categories you may want to reconsider this avenue of investing for the time being:

1. If investing is a supplement to your career
   If you are focused on investing, hire a property manager once you reach 5 units- you will be able to spend your time working at your day job or searching out new property deals instead of dealing with tenants. There are many laws regarding the Fair Housing Act and the Fair Credit Reporting Act- both state and local laws and outsourcing this work to a property manager will help you avoid legal liabilities.

2. If you lack knowledge regarding housing

If you are unfamiliar with the type of housing you have purchased and are going to try to start managing, making a mistake could end up being costly. Also, if you aren't handy with a hammer or able to make basic repairs, you will end up spending more money to hire someone who can.

3. If you want to be a passive investor
   If you are hoping to just collect rent checks from your tenants you will be out of luck, that is unless you decide you can afford to hire a property manager. Being a landlord is a hands-on experience, and if you are not ready to throw yourself into your property full force, you might not be ready to invest in rental properties.

4. If you are not ready to manage your tenants
   Maybe you've decided that you cannot afford to hire a property manager, so you go about acting as the landlord yourself regarding the tenants living in your rental property. If you have one unit it is absolutely doable to manage your own tenants, but as your portfolio begins to increase and your purchase more and more homes, it will be worth your time and energy to get some help with collecting rent and scheduling maintenance and repairs.

Tips for maintaining your rental property

If you get questionable tenants or are just worried about keeping up with your property in general, the following tips will help prevent you from running into costly repairs:

- Restore the roof on the house
  - The roof is one of the most important factors of the house and can be one of its most prominent features. Ensure that the roof is sealed properly and that there are no, or few broken or missing

shingles. While having your entire roof repaired can be costly, it is generally a big ticket item that will last you for many years and will see you through several tenants as well.

- Keep the yard's landscaping neat and tidy
  - Trim overgrown bushes and trees, pull any weeds in the yard and pick up any sticks or leaves that are visible, water any flowers, and complete anything else that will keep the home from becoming an eyesore.
- Make sure smoke and carbon monoxide detectors are working
  - It's stated in many state's building codes that the landlord is in charge of installing and ensure the operation of smoke and carbon monoxide detectors throughout the home. These devices play a large role in the safety of the tenants, and it is very important that they stay in good working condition.
- Unclog the fireplace
  - If you were lucky enough to purchase a home with a fireplace, they need to periodically be cleaned to ensure your house doesn't catch on fire. Take the time to remove dirt, soot, unclog vents or remove other debris that has built up in the chimney.
- Make sure the home's windows are secure
  - Shutters on the outside of a home can wear down, break, or bet damaged by high winds. Windows installed in the home may leak and let rainwater into the home, or if the sealing on them is bad air can leak in and out and wreak havoc on heating and cooling bills.
- Fumigate
  - Cleaning up the yard will help ward off pests, but just to be safe it's a good idea to completely disinfect the premises. Ask around in your area for a solid reference for an extermination service

provider and/or fumigator to work on your property.
- Give the HVAC system a thorough cleaning
    - Keep track of when you change the HVAC filters and note how often the manufacturer suggests changing those. Clean the unit and inspect it for inefficiencies or damages to ensure the AC runs effectively during the hot summer months.

What happens if the property you purchase is not attractive to potential renters?

A property will always be desirable if it has a great walkability score. This score is determined based on the proximity of the home to other amenities such as restaurants, schools, parks, etc. and they can range on a scale from 0 to 10 points. Any home that is given a rating over 70 is considered to be 'walkable'. Buying a home that is considered walkable has several benefits you can point out to potential renters to get them even more excited about the home.

While showing the property let the potential renters know that renting a home in a neighborhood close to the above-listed amenities can increase the number of steps they will take as opposed to living somewhere that they drive instead of walking everywhere. Transportation can also be a very large expense for some people if they have to go far or sit in traffic for long periods of time. If you go to sell a home with a high walkability score, you will find as a seller that these scores are directly linked to higher home values.

If you did your research but somehow you've ended up with a home you cannot rent, you can always relist the property as is, or make some small investments in renovations and repairs to make the property more attractive and hire a real estate agent to not only help you list it but suggest other improvements you could make to increase curb appeal and tenant interest.

What happens if you don't have renter's insurance?

If you own a rental property you need to purchase rental insurance. If your basement floods or something else unexpected happens, don't wait and try to fix things on your own or assume they will fix themselves- call your insurances ASAP and they will help you because that's what you are paying them for. Even if it ends up that the damages are not covered by the insurance, the adjuster can probably help you find local help for other issues that aren't covered.

It's recommended that you survey the damages, even before the crew paid for by insurance arrives to start fixing things. Take photos and samples or any products you may need to replace so you can get a match for the floor, thickness, size, etc. When the contractor or crew arrives don't be afraid to walk through and assess the damages with them so you can ask any questions you may have.

The contractor or crew will approach you with trades, meaning that they will send you a work order to go over and see if you agree with their plan of action including the materials they want to use. Sometimes investors make the mistake of overlooking these trades, but that means you could end up with lower quality materials or with materials that do not match. Keep the information of the contractor that does the work- if you like their quality and price, you can reference them later if you end up running into a similar problem.

Occasionally repairs take longer than expected, so you may need to cut your tenants a break! Crediting rent if the repairs are burdensome can be better for your pocketbook long haul as opposed to finding a brand new tenant. If you call your insurance adjuster, they may agree to reimburse your tenants for half of their rent until the repair work is finished.

Check in on the work regularly to ensure progress is being made and so that you can follow up if anything seems to be done incorrectly or is not getting done at all. During this entire process make sure you keep open communication with your tenants. They will usually be very patient even though this situation can be very disruptive and bothersome to their routine and daily lives. Do not sign off on any of the work until everything is complete, dried, and set. Request that the contractor or crew handles their own cleanup and has installed everything properly and included manuals or demonstrations if necessary.

What to do if you can't find a traditionally listed property within your price range

There are many ways to find properties with great investment potential and that will provide you with great returns. Look into homes that require sweat equity- these will require some major work or simple exterior changes like new paint. Homes in this condition are usually on sale below the real estate market price and may still come in under price after you include the renovation or upgrade costs. To save on labor costs you will be putting in the work and equity into your own home.

If you've been working with a realtor, have them spend some time searching for listings that have been sitting on the market for a while. Even if you are searching for homes on your own, you can usually underbid a house that has been sitting without the fear of offending the homeowner. Take some extra steps on a property that has been stale- ensure that there are no major problems with the house that have caused it to sit for so long.

HUD homes are usually priced to sell, especially if you are going to plan on initially living in the home yourself. These homes are the essentially repossessed after the homeowner defaulted on their FHA loan. The homes are offered to the owner occupants first, and if they can't find the money then investors are allowed to come in after an initial period to bid on the house. Sometimes these homes are dilapidated because the previous owners were unable to afford the home in the first place, or because they chose to neglect the maintenance and upkeep of the property.

Lastly, check out your available options for homes that owned by estates. You will need access to the MLS, so if you don't have access you will probably need to skip this option. A house that someone has inherited and is looking the sell can be a cause of headaches and the owner may take any offer you throw their way to earn some quick cash and get the responsibility of the property off of their hands.

What if you dump a bunch of money into renovations but you still can't rent out the property?

There are home improvements that you will pay for that will be a waste of your money, and they will be other improvements you make that down the road will end up earning you a big repayment. The following are great suggestions for renovations to make that will pay you back instead of costing you money:

1. Kitchen remodel
   Landlords can expect to see back anywhere from 60-120% of their investment in a kitchen remodel as long as you just do the basics and don't go overboard. Ensure that the kitchen matches the rest of the home even after it is completely remodeled.
2. Bathroom addition
   Adding a bathroom can see returns from 80-130% of the amount invested in the addition. If your home only has one bathroom adding a second is a very appealing factor to many renters- how often do we see 3 bed, 1 bath homes where even one more bathroom can make a huge difference in the functionality and appeal of the home.
3. Square footage addition

You can see some of your money back when you put it into adding another room to your home. While this is typically quite expensive, 50-80% of the money spent on this type of work will be recouped as long as you make sure to keep your costs under control.

4. Deck addition

If you own a single-family home, adding a deck into the backyard will make it more appealing to prospective renters and buyers. A landlord can see a whopping 65-90% return on their renovation investment for this small but important addition.

Chapter 5: Managing Your Finances

You either purchased an investment rental property to earn money in the short run, or to earn money and equity in the long run. When you purchase a property, it's a smart idea to set up a bank account just for your rental. If you only own a single rental property at this point, consider setting up a separate checking and savings account at your local bank. Two accounts at a bank you already use make internal transfers simple and there won't be extra fees regarding tax and your mortgage.

Bank accounts

If you have more than one property, having an account for each rental makes more sense and will keep you more organized- open a checking account for the property operations and a savings account to hold tenant security deposits in. While you are opening more accounts, this system makes it simpler to track who paid what each month. Some states require the landlord to hold the security deposit separately, others require interest to be paid- either way, check your local and state laws. When using online banking, you can choose a nickname for each account so you can choose to name them using the property addresses to make the accounts easier to identify. As mentioned in previous chapters, keeping your finances separate and in order will ensure you don't run into any problems down the road, say if a tenant claims they paid rent but you have not record of it.

Bookkeeping and administration

Keeping both a bookkeeping and accounting systems will help you stay organized with your property, finances, and paperwork. Having all of this information is important when it comes time to file your taxes and will allow you to be the most efficient landlord.

Each month reconcile your bank and credit card accounts before the 5th of the month. Use an accounting system, whether it's one you've created yourself, or buy a system like QuickBooks where you can add and correctly label all the transactions. Use this system to also keep all of your important paperwork, receipts, records scanned, and uploaded.

Every quarter and once a year you should file your federal and state payroll reports and make any withholding payments you may owe. Don't forget to file your 1099, 1098, and W2 forms. As the property owner, we suggest you sign all outgoing checks and make any online payments that need to be made, along with entering HUD statements into QuickBooks after you buy or sell a home and conduct a final audit of your financial books before your file your tax return.

If math is not your forte and you have some extra cash, hiring a remote bookkeeper to make sure everything balances out wouldn't be a bad idea. Having your books in order will help you forecast your incoming and outgoing cash flows easier and come tax time everything will be order and the information readily available for when you go to file.

Should you take out a 15-year or 30-year mortgage?

Let's look at a comparison scenario:
You purchased your first home- congratulations! The house cost $184,000 and you put 20% down on the purchase.

30-year mortgage:
4% interest rate
$703 monthly payment
$271,000 in borrowing power
$14,062 in equity in the first 5 years
$107,4000 in total interest paid

15-year mortgage:
3.25% interest rate
$1,034 monthly payment
$184,000 in borrowing power
$41,353 in equity in the first 5 years
$40,548 in total interest paid

Over 30 years a buyer can purchase 47% more house than those that chose a 15-year mortgage but choosing a 15-year mortgage will almost triple your paid equity within 5 years.

Thirty-year mortgages are more common, in fact, they account for more than 80% of all purchase application. Both loan terms are similarly structured, the only difference is the amount of time, meaning a 15-year mortgage will cost you higher monthly payments (but comes with a lower interest rate because they are less risky for the bank). Even though your payment upfront would be larger, a 15-year loan actually saves you the most money long term because you will end up paying drastically less in interest.

Based on a variety of factors, your mortgage payment is broken down into 4 different categories: principal, interest, taxes, and insurance. The principal is the amount of money taken out initially before you include the interest on a loan. The interest is what the bank charges for you to use their borrowed money so that by the end of your loan you will have paid back the principal amount to the bank as well as any interest accrued. Based on your property's value the city you live in will tax you, followed by homeowner's insurance and/or mortgage insurance depending on the situation.

Types of loans

There are several popular options for mortgage loans in the United States, see below for information on qualifications, down payments, and decide on which one is best suited for your investment property.

1. Conventional loan
   -Most common option
   -Usually has the best interest rates
   -Minimum 10% down payment, 20% down is standard
   -This type of loan is perfect for repeat homebuyers

2. Federal Housing Administration (FHA) loan
   -These loans make homeownership affordable
   -Require less money down
   -Have lower credit requirements
   -Minimum 3.5% down payment, 20% down payment is standard
   -This type of loan is perfect for first-time homebuyers

3. Veterans Affairs (VA) loan
   -These loans do not require a down payment without the risk of private mortgage insurance
   -Only available to veterans

4. United States Department of Agriculture (USDA) loan
   -These loans were developed to promote the purchase of rural land
   -No minimum down payment
   -This type of loan is perfect for investors

5. Adjustable Rate Mortgage (ARM) loan
   -These loans start out at rates that are lower than any other option
   -Rate fluctuates with the market (sometimes not for the better)
   -Minimum 10% down payment, 20% down payment is standard
   -This type of loan is perfect for any buyers interested in homeownership

What should you have before you even start investing?

While some people are successful without having the following set up before they buy their first property and start renting it out, it is always a good idea to be as prepared as you can because the unexpected always happens. The following are tips as to how you can be as prepared as you can be regarding your finances in case something comes up:

- Start an emergency fund
  Having a cash store set aside strictly for the purpose of helping you maintain a normal life when an emergency comes up is important. Do not touch this fund as it sits there and gains interest- it will be ready for you when the time comes that you actually need it.

  Maybe you lose your job or the property's water heater tank breaks; having this fund will be a lifesaver. Start with a low goal that will be easily reachable for you within a few months. Break down that goal into smaller monthly or weekly goals, and if you are struggling to find the extra dollars to set aside consider refinancing your credit cards and other loans like your mortgage or even your auto and homeowners' insurance or look at trimming down some of your monthly bills. Another easy solution is to automate your savings by planning weekly or monthly transfers from your checking account to your savings account until it becomes automatic.

- Know, understand, and be able to predict your cash flow
  Create a budget to see how much you can even afford to invest each month in your own savings, and into a property that you will be responsible for managing. This forecast is one of your most important business tools because it will tell you if you can ultimately afford to run your property every day.

The first step is to predict your upcoming sales by using your figures from the following year as a starting point. If you don't have any previous numbers to go off of, use competitor data and industry and area averages- in the end, use your best judgment and estimates to come up with a number. Once you've figured out your projected income for a given month, subtract all of the cash you paid out for your business expenses, loan payments, and anything else that costs money. After subtracting your outflow from your inflow, a positive number is equal to the cash balance that is projected to grow for the month.

- Pay down your debt
  Minimize or completely eliminate any debt you may have, especially focusing on your credit cards. When you stop paying large sums of interest you can see all of that money go back into your pocket. Paying off your debt will also increase your equity so if you are looking at increasing your overall equity aim to pay off those pesky credit cards and student loans.

- Track your net worth

Your net worth represents the sum total of your life's finances reduced down to a few simple numbers. This view will show all of the assets you have accumulated over time and it lists all of your current debts to balance out into a positive or negative number. Decide what you think should be included in your net worth statements, and what kinds of tools you want to use to calculate these numbers. Know your credit score and always be working on improving your number. The most favorable credit score is about a 720, but scores can range anywhere from 300 to 900 points, but most people fall in the 550-750 range. The higher your score the lower the interest rate you are able to qualify for. Free websites like Credit Karma will show you all of your credit scores, as well as what factors are high impact and low impact, and how you can work on improving your score. Setting up an account on Credit Karma will allow you to check your score whenever you want without being penalized. Hard inquiries from credit card companies or banks can ding your credit score, but through this website, checking will not affect your score.

- Outline your goals and priorities
  Why are you investing? When you write them down and look at them frequently they will serve as reminders and motivators for your efforts and actions. Are you purchasing homes to build wealth or are you buying them to help supplement your monthly incoming cash flow? The reasons behind the actions will guide you as you attempt to plan your strategies for purchasing, managing, and selling investment rental properties.

How to purchase a home if you cannot afford to put 20% down

If you are unable to meet the average minimum down payment, you will be required to purchase private mortgage insurance (PMI) even though this insurance only protects the backer of the loan.

With an FHA-backed loan, you won't have to pay a PMI but that type of loan requires a mortgage insurance premium, but you are able to get rid of the premium once you've paid off a certain amount in your home's equity. In the end, it will just depend on how much of a down payment you put down and what the length of your loan term is.

Conventional loans are a little different and are easier to cancel PMI once you reach 20% equity in your home. The loan holder must automatically terminate the PMI without any reminders from you once you've reached that equity amount. This rule is not based on the actual payments you have made, but are tracked by the date by which you should have reached that 20%.

For a USDA or VA loan, there is no requirement for PMI premiums, although a USDA loan requires an annual fee. Since the VA loans are backed by the U.S government, the loans do not require the purchase of PMI.

If you have great credit you may be given the option to buy out of the PMI by agreeing to a slightly higher interest rate. You can also get rid of your PMI through refinancing your home, having a home appraisal, and increasing your home's value through renovations and remodels. If none of these options fit your situation, you may be stuck with paying PMI until you've paid an amount equal to 20% of your home's equity.

Chapter 6: What to Do If You Decide to Sell

Photo by Craig McLachlan on Unsplash

The day you have finally been waiting for is here- you bought the house, rented it out, and now the time has come to pass the property along to its next owner so you can either make a profit off of the sale or you can turn around and reinvest that money into another investment (you won't be taxed if you choose the latter option)!

Choosing a realtor

Choosing a realtor can be just as important as choosing the right tenant, and you should put them through a screening process as well to find a realtor that is the best fit for not only the kind of property you are selling but also for the kind of market you are looking to sell it. The following are some tips to find the perfect realtor to sell your property:

1. Find out who the realtor knows
   Everyone has their own database, influence, personal contacts, and a particular type of client or type of deal they specialize in.

2. Ask them how many properties they own themselves
   Finding a realtor who owns their own rental properties will help you weed out some of the amateurs from seasoned professionals.

3. Choose local
   Realtors that work locally will have guaranteed knowledge of the area and good representation.

4. See if they have a selling strategy
   Can the realtor interpret real estate data? The data is not hard to find but difficult to understand if this is not your field.

5. Test their knowledge about real estate loans
   Ask what they can tell you about real estate loans and the loan process. One of the most time-consuming processes of purchasing a home is the mortgage process, so hiring someone that fully understands the factors involved can help speed up the process and make the process go as smooth as possible for you.

6. Do not focus on their commission
   It may look appealing to choose the realtor that offers the lowest commission fees, but they may point to an issue. We all know that cheapest isn't always best, and purchasing a home is not cheap. The realtor should be firm and you want to feel like you can trust them to protect your best interests.

7. See what the realtor will expect from you as the owner
   If your agent's goal is to present your property in the best way possible, they will need you to cooperate with their efforts.

8. Choose a realtor that asks questions and has good communication
You wouldn't want to hire a realtor that didn't ask you a mountain of questions about your property, questions about your expectations from them, and checking in with you to see what your needs from them are. If an agent seems passive you may want to pass on their services and hire someone who is at least willing to pretend they care about your property and are excited to work with you to sell it.

9. Do not interview competing realtors within the same agency
Let agents know that you are searching around and conducting several interviews but pitting two realtors against each other can lead to a bad outcome on your end. The real estate industry can be very competitive, so don't increase the competition if unnecessary.

10. Check their credentials
Generally speaking, most real estate agents have the same skill set, but like any other professional they can specialize. Did you know that there is a difference between and realtor and a Realtor? Capital 'R' Realtor indicates membership in the National Association of Realtors (NAR) meaning they have taken a pledge to support a real estate code of ethics. Accredited Buyer's Representatives (ABR) who has received further education in how to represent a buyer during a transaction. Certified Residential Specialists (CRS) have received further training in the handling of residential real estate.

11. See if their availability works with your availability
You don't want to have to take time off from your day job to meet up with your real estate agent, so ensure the agent is free at times that work for you.

Staging a home

Before you put your investment rental home on the market it is important to take the time, energy, and money investments into making sure house will quickly sell on the market. Don't go too crazy with colors and patterns in your house- just because you like something doesn't necessarily mean everyone else will like your bright color choices. Neutral colors will help buyers relate to the property and envision their own bright color choices they could see themselves painting the walls in their new home.

Make sure that your storage areas are tidy and functional at the time of the showing. Potential buyers will be poking around the home, looking inside kitchen and bathroom cabinets, and closets too, so make sure you spend some time organizing those areas and uncluttering them so people can see their potential.

If there is furniture in the home ensure that the size and scale of the pieces are conducive to the proportion of the room; these items include but are not limited to the décor pieces, seating, and plants. Rooms that look more empty are better than rooms packed full of furniture because it allows buyers to move freely throughout the house. If you have large pieces of furniture see if you can find somewhere to store them or move them another room where they are a better fit.

Clean everything! Trying to keep your home on a regular cleaning schedule will cut down on the last minute rush to get everything tidied up. You may choose to use a professional cleaner- it can be worth the extra cost depending on your financial and time circumstances. It can hard to tiptoe around your own home, but in the end, it will be less work for you to spend time initially cleaning, and then keep your mess and dishes to a minimum until you've found a potential buyer.

Again, you may love your pet, but that doesn't mean everyone else does (or will); in fact, some people dislike animals and pets altogether so signs of pets in your home like the smell of a litter box, dog hair, or dogs' toys laying all throughout the house may be a turnoff. Another thing to keep in mind is that some people have sensitive allergies or are flat out allergic, so do your best to vacuum up any pet hair and see if you can find a temporary babysitter for your furry friend while the home is being shown.

Details, details, details: it's all in the details. Be upfront with buyers about the flaws in your home, or at least have the issues reflected in the price of the house. The better the quality of the home, the easier it will be for you or your realtor to sell the property. If you have been considering making some upgrades to the property now would be the perfect time to change light fixtures, hardware, water taps and faucets and outdated drapery. You will earn more money as a seller if you make these upgrades up front because you can charge more than the upgrade was actually worth in the total price of the house.

Don't rush the setup process- work on all of the little jobs that need to be completed around the home, and consult your real estate agent about what changes they think will draw buyers to the home: should you repaint the outside a new color? Does that small floor repairs need to be patched up now or after the sale? Spring season brings a lot of competition in the housing market because people are gearing up for summer when it's nice outside and they have extra time to look and buy a new home. If you sell your home in the spring or summer, make sure it stands up to the competition in your area.

Closing costs on your home

The buyer of your home will also pay closing costs, but sellers pay their own costs too. Depending on where you live this cost can be anywhere from 6-10% of the home's sale price. You will not have to pay this money out of your pocket, in fact, it will be taken directly from the profit of your home.

A large portion of seller costs is commission for the real estate agents involved in the sale of your property. This commission is generally negotiable and can vary somewhat depending on the market. Paying off your loan can also cost you a little bit more than continuing to make payments- in some cases, you have assessed a prepayment penalty by paying off the loan before the loan terms are over.

Taxes imposed by the state or local government will be imposed in order to transfer the title from one owner to the home's new owner, cover recording and title insurance fees, or even attorney fees. To break down where the closing costs are going take a look at the following breakdown:

- Seller
    - ½ of title and escrow fees like the transfer tax, title insurance, notary fees, etc.
    - Real estate agent commission
    - Loan payoff including outstanding mortgages
- Buyer
    - ½ of title and escrow fees
    - Lender fees charged for obtaining a mortgage including the appraisal
    - Homeowner's insurance can be paid up front for a year's worth of insurance

Any additional costs at the time of the sale can run between 2-5% of the home's purchase price, but again, buyers and sellers have different costs:

- Seller

- o Optional home warranty, prorated property taxes, brokerage fees, inspections, or prorated HOA fees if applicable
  - o All of these fees are negotiable
- Buyer
  - o Owner's title insurance
  - o Inspection fees
  - o Earnest money
  - o Credit report fee

Conclusion

Photo by Johan Mouchet on Unsplash

Thanks for making it through to the end of *Investing in Rental Properties: Buy, Rent, Sell, Repeat*, and let's hope it was informative and was able to provide you with all of the tools you need to start investing in rental properties. Hopefully, now that you have made your way through the book you have come to terms with the idea that investing is either a good path for you, or you may choose to look at other avenues for investment, but we hope rental properties have piqued your interest. Whether you want to be more hands-on regarding your investments or take a more laid-back approach, real estate has an option for everyone.

The next step is to make sure you've done your research, and begin scouring the market for quality, affordable properties that you can purchase using the tips and strategies we have outlined in this book to purchase your very first investment rental property. We hope that insider information included in this book has left you feeling more confident and inspired to pursue investment opportunities in a real estate sector that interests you; some people prefer residential, but in reality, commercial real estate investing can actually provide larger returns long term.

Whether you are looking to make some quick cash, grow your equity, pay off your debt, or have stable assets for retirement, take a plunge into the real estate world- if you have a solid plan, back up plan, and the determination and motivation to be successful you can earn a great living investing in rental properties. Finally, if you found this book useful in any way, a review on Amazon is always appreciated!

www.ingramcontent.com/pod-product-compliance
Lightning Source LLC
Chambersburg PA
CBHW051326220526
45468CB00004B/1516